Always Follow
Your Dreams,
Wherever They Lead You

Blue Mountain Arts®

Bestselling Books

By Susan Polis Schutz:
To My Daughter, with Love, on the Important Things in Life
To My Son, with Love
I Love You

100 Things to Always Remember... and One Thing to Never Forget
by Alin Austin

Is It Time to Make a Change?
by Deanna Beisser

Trust in Yourself
by Donna Fargo

To the One Person I Consider to Be My Soul Mate
by D. Pagels

For You, Just Because You're Very Special to Me
by Collin McCarty

Chasing Away the Clouds
by Douglas Pagels

Anthologies:
42 Gifts I'd Like to Give to You
Always Believe in Yourself and Your Dreams
Creeds of Life, Love, & Inspiration
Follow Your Dreams Wherever They Lead You
For You, My Daughter
Friends Are Forever
Friends for Life
I Love You, Mom
I'm Glad You Are My Sister
The Joys and Challenges of Motherhood
The Language of Recovery ...and Living Life One Day at a Time
Life Can Be Hard Sometimes ...but It's Going to Be Okay
Marriage Is a Promise of Love
May You Always Have an Angel by Your Side
Mottos to Live By
Take Each Day One Step at a Time
Teaching and Learning Are Lifelong Journeys
There Is Greatness Within You, My Son
These Are the Gifts I'd Like to Give to You
Think Positive Thoughts Every Day
Thoughts of Friendship
Thoughts to Share with a Wonderful Teenager
To My Child
True Friends Always Remain in Each Other's Heart
With God by Your Side ...You Never Have to Be Alone
Words of Love
You're Just like a Sister to Me

Always Follow
Your Dreams,
Wherever They Lead You

Special Edition
A Blue Mountain Arts® Collection

Blue Mountain Press™

SPS Studios, Inc., Boulder, Colorado

Library of Congress Catalog Card Number: 85-72417
ISBN: 0-88396-234-9

The publisher wishes to thank Susan Polis Schutz for permission to reprint the following poems in this publication: "This life is yours...." Copyright © 1978 by Continental Publications. And for "You Deserve the Best," "I know that lately...," "Believe in Your Dreams," and "Follow Your Dreams." Copyright © 1982, 1983, 1984, 1985 by Stephen Schutz and Susan Polis Schutz. All rights reserved.

ACKNOWLEDGMENTS appear on page 92.

Certain trademarks are used under license.

Manufactured in China
Tenth Printing: December 2001

 This book is printed on recycled paper.

This book is printed on fine quality, laid embossed, 80 lb. paper. This paper has been specially produced to be acid free (neutral pH) and contains no groundwood or unbleached pulp. It conforms with all the requirements of the American National Standards Institute, Inc., so as to ensure that this book will last and be enjoyed by future generations.

SPS Studios, Inc.

P.O. Box 4549, Boulder, Colorado 80306

CONTENTS

Reaching for Rainbows

If we don't ever take chances,
   we won't reach the rainbows.
If we don't ever search,
   we'll never be able to find.
If we don't attempt to get over
   our doubts and fears,
   we'll never discover how wonderful
      it is to live without them.
If we don't go beyond difficulty,
   we won't grow any stronger.
If we don't keep our dreams alive,
   we won't have our dreams any longer.

But . . .
if we can take a chance now and then,
seek and search, discover and dream,
grow and go through each day
with the knowledge that
we can only take as much as we can give,
and we can only get as much out of life
   as we allow ourselves to live . . .

Then . . .
we can be truly happy.
We can realize a dream or two along the way,
and we can make a habit of
   reaching out for rainbows
      and coloring our lives
            with wonderful days.

— Collin McCarty

Reach for Your Star . . .

Do not take anything as being forever,
because forever is only as long as today.
Know that the people who are the richest
are not those who have the most,
    but those who need the least.
That we are at our strongest when life
    is at its worst,
and at our weakest when life no longer
    offers a challenge.
That it is wiser not to expect, but to hope,
for in expecting you ask for disappointment,
whereas in hoping you invite surprise.
That unhappiness doesn't come from
    not having something you want,

but from the lack of something inside
 that you need.
That there are things to hold and things
 to let go,
and letting go doesn't mean you lose,
 but that you acquire that which
has been waiting around the corner.
Most of all . . .
remember to use your dreams as a
 way of knowing yourself better,
and as an inspiration to reach for your star.

     — Nancye Sims

Don't Ever Stop Dreaming Your Dreams

Don't ever try to understand everything —
    some things will just never make sense.
Don't ever be reluctant to show your feelings —
    when you're happy, give into it!
    When you're not, live with it.
Don't ever be afraid to try to make things better —
    you might be surprised at the results.
Don't ever take the weight of the world
    on your shoulders.
Don't ever feel threatened by the future —
    take life one day at a time.
Don't ever feel guilty about the past —
    what's done is done. Learn from any mistakes
    you might have made.
Don't ever feel that you are alone —
    there is always somebody there for you
    to reach out to.
Don't ever forget that you can achieve
    so many of the things you can imagine —
    imagine that! It's not as hard as it seems.
Don't ever stop loving,
    don't ever stop believing,
        don't ever stop dreaming your dreams.

— Laine Parsons

As you press on toward your
dreams, remember this . . .

To solve each problem one at a time;
to take each day as it comes.
To stick to your goals, no matter
   what happens,
and press on toward your dreams.
To keep your attention focused on
   the future,
as you consider the solutions at hand.
To look for the bright side,
even though it may be temporarily
   covered by a cloud.
To smile often, even when a frown
   feels more natural.

To think of those you love,
    and know that they love you, too.
No matter how difficult it may seem,
you have within you the power,
    the ability,
        and the knowledge
to make things better.

— Lindsay Newman

You can be more than you dreamed . . .

Believe that you are far more
   wonderful than you ever dared
      to imagine . . . because you are.
Believe that you can be more
   than you have ever dreamed . . .
      because you can.
Believe that you have more courage
   than you can see . . . because you do.
Believe that you are stronger
   than your fears have allowed you
   to know . . . because you are.
Believe that you can love more fully
   than you ever thought . . . because
      you are able to.
Believe that you are truly more unique
   and special than you have ever
   allowed yourself to acknowledge . . .
      because you really are.

Believe it . . . if it's the
   last thing you do.

    Believe it . . .
      because it's true.

— Sue Mitchell

Believe in Your Dreams

Believe in yourself
Get to know yourself
what you can do and what you cannot do
for only you can make your
life happy

Believe in work, learning and achieving
as a way of reaching
your goals
and being successful

Believe in creativity
as a means of expressing
your true feelings
and as a way of
being spontaneous

Believe in appreciating life
Be sure to have fun every day
and to enjoy
the beauty in the world

Believe in loving
Love your friends, love your family
love yourself, love your life

Believe in long-term relationships
Be sure the people are worthy of your love
and be very honest with them

Believe in your dreams
and your dreams can become
a reality

— Susan Polis Schutz

Never stop believing
in your dreams . . .

Goals are dreams and wishes
that are not easily reached.
You have to work hard to
obtain them,
never knowing when
or where
you will reach your goal.

But keep trying!
Do not give up hope.
And most of all . . .
never stop
believing in yourself.

For within you
there is someone
special . . .

someone wonderful
and successful.
No matter what you achieve,
as long as you want it
and it makes you
happy,

you are a success.

— Rosemary DePaolis

My Favorite Wishes for You

For you to always find whatever you seek from life, and more: not just happiness, but joy, and a life that is better than you ever imagined before.

For you to feel safe and secure; for you to feel strong and self-assured, fully able to enjoy the blessings of this day and all your beautiful tomorrows.

For you to always take care, to feel good about yourself within; for you to be well and to always feel as wonderful as you always look to me.

For you to remember that my light will
    always shine for you; that you'll never
    be without a dear friend to talk to;
    you'll never be without someone who
    loves you and cherishes the person you are.

You'll never be without someone
    who hopes for the best
        in everything you do.
You'll never be without me
    wishing nothing but good things
                for you.

— Collin McCarty

Don't ever give up
   your dreams . . .
and never leave
   them behind.
Find them; make them yours,
and all through your life,
cherish them,
   and never let them go.

— Elisa Costanza

It's okay to be afraid sometimes,
        but always believe in your dreams . . .

It's okay to be afraid
of the things we don't understand.
It's okay to feel anxious
when things aren't working our way.
It's okay to feel lonely . . .
even when you're with other people.
It's okay to feel unfulfilled
because you know something is missing
(even if you're not sure what it is).
It's okay to think and worry and cry.

It's okay to do
whatever you have to do, but
just remember, too . . .
that eventually you're going to
adjust to the changes life brings your way,
and you'll realize that
it's okay to love again and laugh again,
and it's okay to get to the point where
the life you live
is full and satisfying and good to you . . .
and it will be that way
because you made it that way.

— Laine Parsons

You are a wonderful,
     worthy and loveable person.
Appreciate that
about yourself.
No one has ever been,
or ever will be,
quite like you.
You are an individual,
     an original,
and all those things that make you
uniquely you
are deserving of love
          and praise.

— Peter A. McWilliams

I Believe in Your Dreams

Would it help
for you to know
how much I believe in you?
When things are hard,
please remember that.
Remember that you have someone
who is always on your side,
walking beside you
whether you win or lose,
whether you're happy or sad.
In the same way that I believe
that a sunny day lies ahead,
I believe in you.

— Sheri Carmon

As you reach out for your dreams,
remember that you are loved . . .

When the road seems too long
When darkness sets in
When everything turns out wrong
And you can't find a friend
Remember — you are loved

When smiles are hard to come by
And you're feeling down
When you spread your wings to fly
And can't get off the ground
Remember — you are loved

When time runs out before you're through
And it's over before you begin
When little things get to you
And you just can't win
Remember — you are loved

When your loved ones are far away
And you are on your own
When you don't know what to say
When you're afraid of being alone
Remember — you are loved

When your sadness comes to an end
And everything is going right
May you think of your family and friends
And keep their love in sight
A thank-you for being loved

May you see the love around you
In everything you do
And when troubles seem to surround you
May all the love shine through
You are blessed — you are loved

— Roger Pinches

Sometimes the world
        seems so cold.
There are moments when
    you try your best,
and even that isn't good enough.
You yearn for the best
    life has to offer,
but you wonder if it will ever appear.

But *you have to keep believing* . . .
    you have to remember
that things *will* get better,
    that you will find strength,
        and you have to
            believe in yourself . . .

        the way that I
            believe in you.

— Gina Bowie

Gentle Words of Encouragement

Spend every day preparing for the next.

As you reach forward with one hand, accept
the advice of those who have gone
before you, and in the same manner
reach back with the other hand to those
who follow you; for life is a fragile chain
of experiences held together by love.
Take pride in being a strong link in that
chain. Discipline yourself, but do not be
harsh. The pleasures of life are yours to
be taken. Share them with others, but
always remember that you, too, have
earned the right to partake.

Know those who love you; love is the finest
of all gifts and is received only to be
given. Embrace those who truly love
you; for they are few in a lifetime.

Then return that love tenfold, radiating it
from your heart to fill their lives as sunlight
warms the darkest corners of the earth.
Love is a journey, not a destination;
travel its path daily. Do this and your
troubles will be as fleeting as footprints
in the sand. When loneliness is your
companion and all about you seem to be
gone, pause and listen, for the sound of
loneliness is silence, and in silence we
hear best. Listen well, and your
moments of silence will always be
broken by the gentle words of
encouragement spoken by those of us
who love you.

— Tim Murtaugh

You Deserve the Best

A person will get only what he wants
You must choose your goals carefully
Know what you like
and what you do not like
Be critical about what you can do well
and what you cannot do well
Choose a career or lifestyle that interests you
and work hard to make it a success
Enter a relationship that is worthy of everything
you are physically and mentally
Be honest with people, help them if you can
but don't depend on anyone to make life easy
or happy for you
Only you can do that for yourself
Strive to achieve all that you like
Find happiness in everything you do
Love with your entire being
Make a triumph
of every aspect
of your life

— Susan Polis Schutz

A Word of Advice

I want to tell you
to go ahead and reach out
    for what you want.

I want to tell you
to go ahead and try;
    try to make the things happen
        that you want to happen.

Along the way
there may be some pain,
disappointment and doubt,
but if you never try,
you'll never know
what might have been,
and you'll always wonder
"what if" and "if only . . ."

Even though you
might be scared,
you'll have reason to be
proud of yourself
and glad that you dared

to reach out
for the dreams
that only you
can make come true.

— Marsha Reid

Learning isn't easy . . .
frustration tends to
    set in quickly.
You hurt.
You feel defeated.
You want to give up —
    to quit.
You want to walk away
    and pretend it doesn't
        matter.
But you won't,
because you're not a loser —
    you're a fighter.

We all have to lose sometimes
    before we can win,
we have to cry sometimes
    before we can smile.

We have to hurt
    before we can be strong.
But if you keep on working
        and believing,
you'll have victory
    in the end.

— Ann Davies

Never give up your dreams.
Imagine what you want for tomorrow.
Feel it, sense it,
fill your soul with it.

Dare the impossible
because deep down inside
you know it can be done.
Be unafraid, but not foolish.
Have courage, and balance it
    with strength.
Be confident in who you are.
Don't be afraid to grow.

Above all, know what
your inner spirit desires.

Listen to your hopes and dreams . . .
  to the unseen element inside you,
  to the sounds that are beyond hearing,
  to the one part of you that
    knows no boundaries
  and that walks hand in hand with you
    through your life.

Never give up your dreams,
for they were meant
    to come true.

— P.F. Heller

In Our Lives . . .

In our lives there are things
we may never understand,
no matter how hard we try.
Still . . . we must do our best,
    and know we'll always get by.

In our lives are desires
we may never realize,
regardless of how much we hope.
Still . . . we must go on, believing
that the things meant to be . . . will be,
    and that all things are possible.

In our lives there are many things
that we can change and control
    as we choose; other things
        are less affected by us.
It is up to us
    to set the stage
        for good things to come our way.

For in our lives,
in the course of our days,
no matter how sunny or gray,
   there is a wonderful opportunity
         given to each . . .

If only we can believe and remember
that — even though our dreams
   may sometimes seem far away —
   they're never out of reach.

— Collin McCarty

Success begins with a single step
that takes you as far as your
determination and dedication
want to go.
Others may help you along the way,
but in the end,
it's your wanting to get there badly
    enough
that completes the journey.

Success doesn't come fast,
nor does it come easily.
There will be times when you'll ask
yourself if it's really worth the
    struggle,
and you'll wonder if you'll ever get
    there.

But you will, my friend,
if you remain strong
and refuse to let any obstacles
stand in the way of achieving your
      dreams.

If you believe firmly in what you
      are doing
and patiently keep taking those tiny
      steps,
you will get there and know
the thrill that comes with meeting
a challenge and winning.

— Nancye Sims

This life is yours
Take the power
to choose what you want to do
and do it well
Take the power
to love what you want in life
and love it honestly
Take the power
to walk in the forest
and be a part of nature
Take the power
to control your own life
No one else can do it for you
Take the power
to make your life happy

— Susan Polis Schutz

I know you are making some very
  big changes.
Maybe they are not easy,
  perhaps even a little scary.
But changes are good,
  and they make life richer.
So take those giant steps for
  your inner self
that wants to reach higher,
and all of us who love you
  will rejoice in your happiness
    and your growing.

             — Dawn Abraham

There are times in every life
when we feel hurt or alone . . .
But I believe that these times
when we feel lost
and all around us seems
        to be falling apart
    are really bridges of growth.
We struggle and try to recapture
    the security of what was,
        but almost in spite of ourselves
we emerge on the other side
with a new understanding,
    a new awareness,
    a new strength.
It is almost as though
    we must go through the pain
        and the struggle
            in order to grow
and reach new heights.

— Sue Mitchell

Things won't always be easy
          on your journey of life.

There will be new challenges,
and the right path won't always
          be easy to spot.
Just remember to follow your heart,
    and build on the lessons
          you've already learned.

And remember, too, that you
    don't have to always be strong.
It's only natural to feel confused
    and afraid sometimes,
but know that you have the resources
    to overcome any obstacle
that stands between you
          and your dreams.

And . . . if you ever need someone
    to lean on,
        to share your fears with,
          to share your dreams with . . .

          remember that I'm here.

— Stacey Hoffman

One day at a time —
this is enough.
Do not look back
and grieve over
    the past,
for it is gone;
and do not be troubled
about the future,
for it has not yet come.
Live in the present,
and make it so beautiful
that it will be worth
    remembering.

— Ida Scott Taylor

I know this time in your life
is as confusing for you as it is
    exciting.
Before, there was a safe path for
    you to follow,
and now suddenly there are unfamiliar
    curves,
and you're unsure about which way
    to go.
I understand your feelings.

I wish there were something I could
    say or do to erase your fears,
    to lessen your confusion,
but having been there myself,
    I know there isn't.

This time is only a bridge you must
    cross to get to the other side.
Once there, you'll look back at this
    crossing with smiles and laughter,
and with memories you'll cherish
    for the rest of your life.

Meanwhile . . .
Do whatever you can to
    make this time in your life
a time you'll look back upon
    as one of the best.

— Nancye Sims

You have powers you never dreamed of. You can do things you never thought you could do. There are no limitations in what you can do except the limitations in your own mind as to what you cannot do.
Don't think you cannot.
Think you can.

— Darwin P. Kingsley

Each day we live is an opportunity
to discover a completely new world.

This day has never before been seen;
it arrives fresh each morning,
offering all the hope and promise
of a fulfilling future . . .

A world where special dreams
meet successful achievement,
where challenges are the inspiration
for spiritual growth and insight,
a world where love, in all its
diversity of expression, is
a constant force in our lives.

A new beginning, a new world
of our hopes and dreams,
is the potential each day offers us . . .
a potential we each deserve,
and have the talent, to achieve.

— Edmund O'Neill

Past mistakes don't have to
cloud up your future;
neither do they have to
prevent you from trying new things.
Only if you hold on to them
 will they get in your way.

You have been courageous enough
to risk making a mistake.
Praise yourself for your strength.
Remind yourself that this mistake
was most likely a necessary step
for you to take in order to gain
more understanding about life
and your place in it.

Then look to the future
and realize that your dreams
are still there.
They may have changed,
but they are still your dreams.

— Donna Levine

Be the Best You Can Be

Always have faith that tomorrow will be better than today. Remember, optimism is always a brighter window to look out on the world than is pessimism and despair. Always believe in the good of people; the capacity of the human spirit for accomplishing good is boundless. Be the best you can be; it will not only help you to grow as a person, but will inspire others to do the same. Leave your heart open to forgive others, for a time will come when you, too, will seek the healing forgiveness of a kindred soul. Strive for the things that touch the heart, for only then can you achieve the peace and contentment that go into shaping a happy life. Always be true to the moment at hand, for there are moments in life that, when they pass through the affections of the heart, will leave within us memories that glow as bright as any star that smiles down at us from above. And as you pass through this world, may you leave a trail of peace and goodwill wherever you go, and may those whose lives you have touched along the way feel richer of heart because you have touched their hearts with the friendship in your own.

— Daniel Haughian

Listen to Your Heart

We all want to make things better
in our lives, but lots of times we just
don't know where or when to begin.
Sometimes we are troubled about something
deep inside, and we are afraid
of dealing with our problems
   because we've been hurt before,
      and we remember what hurts can bring.
Making things better involves changing . . .
but change isn't such a terrible thing.

Life isn't always easy. No one ever
promised that it would be. But it
can be wonderful at times, and it
is up to us to make those times happen.
Where? Beginning within.
   When? With the dawn of each new day.
     How? Listen to your heart . . .
        and it really will show you the way.

— Collin McCarty

A New Hope

We will probably never understand
all of life's disappointments,
but each disappointment is a chance
to draw closer to yourself —
find your own strengths,
and realize that you can make it
even when the dream shatters.
You begin to see that when one dream ends,
you can always begin to dream again —
and for as long as you can dream,
you can find new places in life,
set new goals, and build a new and
more solid foundation, with new and
better expectations of what life can offer . . .

With each disappointment you can
better find yourself,
and see more clearly
just how strong a person
you're becoming.

— Sharon Davis

You are struggling . . .
   I see it,
   I feel it,
   I hurt for you.
But I must tell you, dear friend,
I believe with all my heart
that you will emerge
  somehow wiser, stronger,
   and more aware.
Hold on to that thought,
    tuck it away in a
    corner of your heart
    until the hurt melts enough
    for the learning to have
    meaning.

— Sue Mitchell

I know you're going
to make it . . .
It may take time
and hard work
You may become frustrated
and at times you'll feel
like giving up
Sometimes you may even
wonder if it's really
worth it
But I have confidence
in you,
and I know you'll make it,
if you try.

— amanda pierce

The First Step

There is a world out there
        waiting for you . . .
a world
that you've only
        dreamed of.

But you're the only one
who can make it come true.
Use the strength you've got inside you
   to open the door.
Use the courage you hold deep within
   to take a step
      in the right direction.
Use the knowledge that you really
   will make it if you try.

Just take the first step,
in the direction of whatever you want to do,
and soon your fears will all be past;
you will put them behind you and know
   you made it through.

Just take the first step . . .
            and then another . . .
   and before you know it
      a more wonderful world
         will begin to show itself to you.

— Collin McCarty

In This Moment in Time

Reach. Strive. And you will succeed.
Try . . . but don't try too hard.
   Some of the best things come naturally.
Give . . . but don't give beyond your means.
   Save some strength and some quiet
   time for yourself.
Question . . . but don't question everything.
   Some problems have no answers.
Attempt . . . but don't try to conquer
   everything at once. Go slowly,
   discovering and growing along the way.
Trust in doing the right thing, even if
   it may seem wrong at the time.

Believe in your inner strength, even if
   you don't feel very strong all the time.
Live your life and give your best,
   and try each and every day
     to keep in mind . . .

that to truly enjoy
   this moment in time,
all you really need to do
   is to reach out for your dreams . . .
     and let them reach out to you.

— Laine Parsons

To live life to its fullest . . .

Is to look forward to each day
   as a new adventure,
to learn from your mistakes,
   to grow,
to appreciate the beauty in
   this world,
to love yourself, so you can
   love others,
to accept differences without
   criticism and appreciate them
   for what they are,
to strive to be a better person,
to set your goals and work for them,

to find joy in giving and loving
and sharing and caring,
to find peace within yourself,
so that you can appreciate the
world around you,
to spend time with family and friends,
to make new friends,
to thank God each new day, and
to dream of each new tomorrow
as another new adventure.

— Debbie Avery

I know that lately you
have been having problems
and I just want you to know
that you can rely on me for anything
you might need
But more important
keep in mind at all times
that you are very capable
of dealing with any complications
that life has to offer
So
do whatever you must
feel whatever you must
and keep in mind at all times
that we all
grow wiser and
become more sensitive and
are able to enjoy life more
after we go through
hard times

— Susan Polis Schutz

Go After Our Dreams . . .

We live in a world that sometimes
lacks understanding and forgiveness.
There are times when nothing seems
to make sense, and times when
    it never will.
Sometimes the most we can hope for
is an inner patience . . . knowing that
    the winds of change
        will eventually send a
           fresh new breeze
              into our lives.
Sometimes the most we can hope for
is someone who understands . . .
who touches us and tells us —

without need for touching or words —
that it will be okay,
and we know that it will be
   because they are here for us.

And sometimes we just need to remember,
no matter what the world sends our way,
that it is so important to go after
our dreams, and to reach for our goals . . .
never forgetting that,
   with every smile and effort and hope,
      we'll get a little closer
         . . . every day.

                              — Collin McCarty

Follow Your Dreams

I wish for you, my friend
to have
   people to love
   everyone think about you the way I do
   blue skies on clear days
   exciting things to do
   easy solutions to any problems
   knowledge to make the right decisions
   strength in your values
   laughter and fun
   goals to pursue
   happiness in all that you do
I wish for you, my friend
to have
   beautiful experiences
   each new day
   as you follow
   your dreams

— Susan Polis Schutz

Promises to keep as I
pursue my dreams . . .

To not worry so much
about things that are beyond my control;
To not try to please everybody;
To remember that I'm never really alone,
and that dear friends and precious
loved ones will always be beside me;
To have good thoughts,
and chase away the bad;
To keep my sense of humor
(even when that's hard to do);
To not lose faith that
things will turn out okay;
To not lose track of
what is important, and what isn't;
To always try to do the best I can
at whatever I am doing;
To not let yesterday or tomorrow
weigh me down;

To remember that the most important
    day of my life is the day
    that dawned this morning, and that
    the rewards I will receive today
    depend so much on me —
    on my outlook, on my inner peace,
    on never giving up, but always
        reaching out;
To let go of my fears;
    to hold on to my dreams.

— Collin McCarty

I believe that through
every storm or problem we face in life,
the solutions are ours to find.
It takes a belief in ourselves
and in our ability to handle
the situations we must deal with.

We must accept our problems
and work through them. It won't
always be easy, but a positive
outlook will lighten the load.
Finding answers and solutions
won't be an easy task, but then
neither is life.

But we broaden our horizons by
the challenges we face, and each
day we must remember all the
possibilities that life has just
offered us.
Believe and achieve.

— Sherrie Householder

It's natural to feel disappointed
   when things don't go your way
It's easy to think . . .
   "I can't do it, so why try?"
But, no matter how scared you are
      of making a mistake
or how discouraged you may become,
Never give up . . .
because if you don't try and
if you don't go after what you
   want in life,
it won't come to you,
and you'll be forced to accept
   things that you know could
      be better . . .

Success is not measured by
whether you win or
whether you fail —
there's always a little bit
of success, even if things
don't go your way —
What's important is that you'll
feel better about yourself,
for the simple reason
that you tried.

— amanda pierce

Do the Best You Can

This I pray for you, my friend —
That you strive to be all that you can be,
　　yet never become a copy of another
That you realize your own unique qualities,
　　and all that makes you special
That you open your eyes to the beauty
　　in each day
That you reach out to others less fortunate
　　than you
That, by giving, you learn the joy of
　　receiving
That you let go of the sadness of the past,
　　yet always remember the good moments
That you learn to accept life as it is,
　　even with its problems and disappointments
For life is meant to be enjoyed
　　and, at times, endured, but never taken
　　for granted
And I pray that you will be aware at all
　　times that you are one special person,
　　among all special persons
And do the best you can.

— Rhoda-Katie Hannan

Keep Your Dreams Alive

Nobody ever said it would be easy . . .
experiencing life,
   discovering that it has
         downs as well as ups.
At least the disappointments
don't last very long
and don't affect you as much
when you know that no matter what —
      you have much to look forward to.

               You really do!

Think . . .
   think of yourself as a seeker —
   see the process of discovery
      as endless, and yet
            find peace in that fact.

Be . . .
   be a lover — of life,
    of people, of nature, and
     of the nuances unfolding within.

Reach . . .
   reach out and realize your goals;
      stretch yourself, take risks,
         and try to understand
            and extend your capabilities.

Listen . . .
   listen more and more
      to your intuition, and know
         that it holds a wonderful wisdom.

Explore . . .
   explore and rediscover
      the creativity you felt as a child,
   and envision anew those things
      you may have stopped seeing
         on the way to growing up.

Remember . . .
   remember to keep your dreams alive,
      and happiness will always be
         in your heart.

                              — Sue Mitchell

You Have Your Own
Special Dreams

In the dream of your next new day,
wake up and realize
    what a wonderful person you are.

Remember that you are loved,
    and that you have good friends
        who will always be beside you,
    and that you have your own
        special dreams . . . always there
            to reach out for and to guide you.

You're such a precious person;
    so believe in yourself and don't
        ever quit. You're a winner in my book,
        and the world is lucky to have you
            as a part of it.

— Collin McCarty

There's something rare and special
about a person who always makes you
    feel good — without even trying.
There's something magical in
    a smile that talks.
There's a lingering warmth in laughter
    that comes so easy that nothing else
    seems to matter.
The ability to touch people without
    having to reach out —
    a simple understanding of hearts.
There's nothing more refreshing
    than coming across such a person
    in your life —
And nothing so appreciated as being able
    to call them your friend.

— Lynn Barnhart

Each of us has a dream . . .

Deep within our hearts,
each of us carries the seed
of a secret dream,
special and unique to each individual.
Sometimes another person
can share that dream
and help it grow to fulfillment;
other times, the dream remains
a solitary pursuit, known only
to the seeker. But secret or shared,
no matter what it might be,
a dream is a potential which
should never be discouraged. For
each of us also carries within ourselves
a light which can cause the seed
to grow and blossom
        into beautiful reality . . .
that same light I've seen shine
so clearly in you.

— Edmund O'Neill

Go Confidently in the Direction
of Tomorrow

Even when things have gone
about as wrong as they can go,
don't get discouraged.

The old expression about
"If you fall off a horse,
the best thing to do is to
    get right back on,"
has a lot of wisdom written into it.
It's the same with life.
Sometimes we go riding along,
having the time of our life,
when all of a sudden
    the unexpected happens
and turns our world around.

But it's then . . . when we're feeling
anxious and hurt and afraid . . .
that we need to look deep inside
and see — that we can either
    stay in the place where we fell,
or we can get right back up
    and go confidently
        in the direction of tomorrow.

And remember . . .
it's okay to stay down as long as it takes
    to recover from each and every fall.
But don't ever be afraid of getting up
    and beginning again just as soon
        as you feel the need . . .

    because "next time" might very well be
        the time that you succeed.

— Collin McCarty

ACKNOWLEDGMENTS

We gratefully acknowledge the permission granted by the following authors to reprint their works.

Nancye Sims for "Reach for Your Star . . . ," "Success begins with a single step," and "I know this time in your life." Copyright © Nancye Sims, 1985. All rights reserved. Reprinted by permission.

Sherrie Householder for "I believe that through every storm." Copyright © Sherrie Householder, 1985. All rights reserved. Reprinted by permission.

Sue Mitchell for "There are times." Copyright © Sue Mitchell, 1981. And for "You are struggling." Copyright © Sue Mitchell, 1983. And for "Believe that you are far" and "Keep Your Dreams Alive." Copyright © Sue Mitchell, 1985. All rights reserved. Reprinted by permission.

Elisa Costanza for "Don't ever give up your dreams." Copyright © Elisa Costanza, 1981. All rights reserved. Reprinted by permission.

Peter A. McWilliams for "You are a wonderful." Copyright © Peter A. McWilliams, 1981. All rights reserved. Reprinted by permission.

Gina Bowie for "Sometimes the world." Copyright © Gina Bowie, 1984. All rights reserved. Reprinted by permission.

Tim Murtaugh for "Gentle Words of Encouragement." Copyright © Tim Murtaugh, 1983. All rights reserved. Reprinted by permission.

Marsha Reid for "A Word of Advice." Copyright © Marsha Reid, 1985. All rights reserved. Reprinted by permission.

Ann Davies for "Learning isn't easy . . ." Copyright © Ann Davies, 1983. All rights reserved. Reprinted by permission.